Book 3

English Headwork

Deborah Waters and Chris Culshaw

Oxford University Press   1986

Acknowledgements

The publishers would like to thank the following for permission to reproduce photographs:

BMW (GB) Ltd. p. 36 (8); Bruce Coleman Ltd./Hans Reinhard p. 26;
Gerald Duckworth Ltd. p. 4; Heron Suzuki GB Ltd, p. 36 (5);
Honda (UK) Ltd. p. 36 (2 and 7); Kawasaki Information Service p. 36 (1 and 6);
Mitsui Machinery Sales (UK) Ltd. p. 36 (3 and 4);
The Photo Source Ltd. p. 28.

Illustrations are by
Peter Bailey, Gecko Ltd., Vanessa Luff, Trevor Ridley,
Paul Sawyers, Ursula Sieger, Kate Simpson,
Barrie Thorpe and Shaun Williams.

Oxford University Press, Walton Street, Oxford OX2 6DP

Oxford New York Toronto
Delhi Bombay Calcutta Madras Karachi
Petaling Jaya Singapore Hong Kong Tokyo
Nairobi Dar es Salaam Cape Town
Melbourne Auckland

and associated companies in
Beirut Berlin Ibadan Nicosia

Oxford is a trade mark of Oxford University Press
© Oxford University Press 1986

First published 1986

ISBN 0 19 833378 1

The crossword on page 46 may be photocopied for classroom use.

All rights reserved. No other part of this publication may be reproduced, stored in a retrieval system, or transmitted, in any form or by any means electronic, mechanical, photocopying, recording, or otherwise, without the prior permission of Oxford University Press

This book is sold subject to the condition that it shall not, by way of trade or otherwise, be lent, re-sold, hired or otherwise circulated, without the publisher's prior consent in any form of binding or cover other than that in which it is published and without a similar condition including this condition being imposed on the subsequent purchaser

Typeset by Oxford Publishing Services
Printed by R. J. Acford, Chichester

Contents

1	**Inventions**	4
2	**Mill Street**	14
3	**Giants**	24
4	**Motorbike**	36
5	**Leisure**	46
Talking Points		63
Note for Teachers		64

INVENTIONS

Inventions

The Anti-litter Machine

What to do
Look at the picture and fill in the missing words.

The anti-litter machine is made from a car with a wooden ___1___ in front and a tower on top. Two ___2___ sit in the car. They drive the car.

There is a ___3___ of gum above the roller. Gum drips onto the wooden roller. It is ___4___ all over the wooden roller. When the anti-litter machine drives over some rubbish it ___5___ on to the roller. There is a man sitting on a chair on the ___6___ of the car. He holds two forks. He takes the ___7___ off the roller with the forks and throws them in a bin behind him.

Two men ___8___ in the tower. One man has a pair of ___9___. He looks for anyone dropping litter. He tells the other man who pulls a ___10___ which rings a bell. If the bell on the ___11___ rings the driver steers to the right. If the bell on the ___12___ rings he steers to the left.

What to do next
Design a fantastic machine for rescuing cats from high buildings.
Draw and label it.
Write a story about your machine.

Inventions

Everyday Inventions

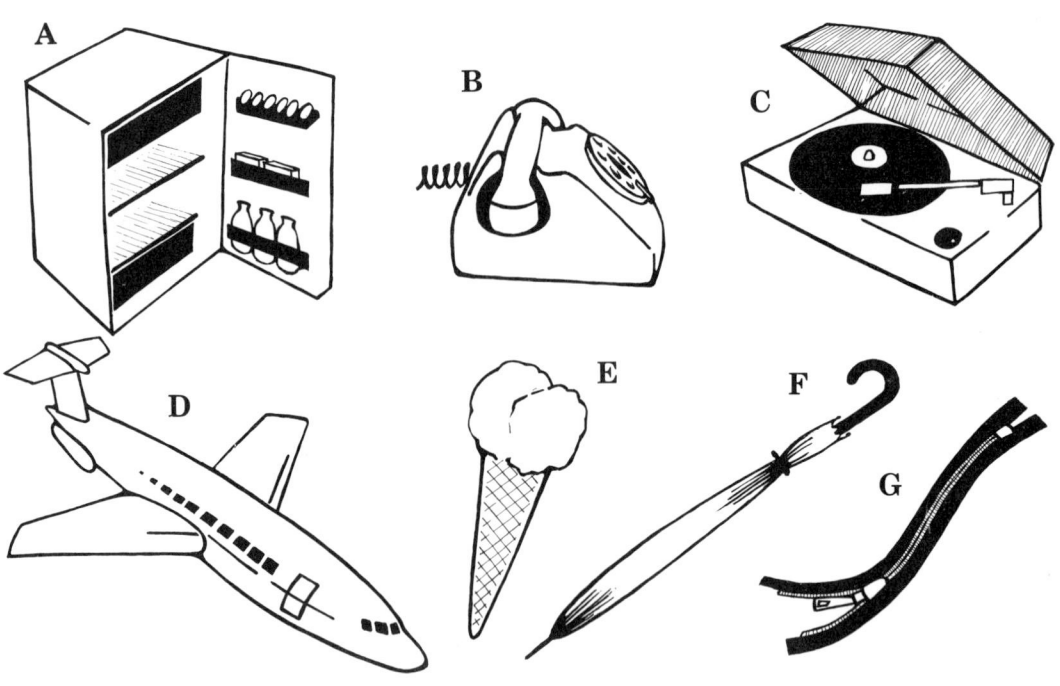

What to do

Match the people with the inventions they might find useful.
Some may use more than one invention.

1. Mark is a cleaner in a large carpet shop.
2. Emily lives alone. She doesn't have many visitors. Sometimes she gets lonely.
3. Colette is a secretary. She has to type many letters.
4. Graham works as a nurse in the hospital.
5. Marie is blind. She loves reading.
6. Paul lives in Jamaica. He is a chef.
7. Lesley is a business woman. She has to travel all over the world.
8. Carl is in the traffic police.
9. Gerry stays at home to look after his one year old daughter. She is always getting her clothes dirty.
10. Beth was paralysed from the waist down in a road accident.
11. Kamala is short sighted. She hates wearing glasses.
12. Rashid works in the evenings. He loves watching TV but he misses his favourite programmes.

Inventions

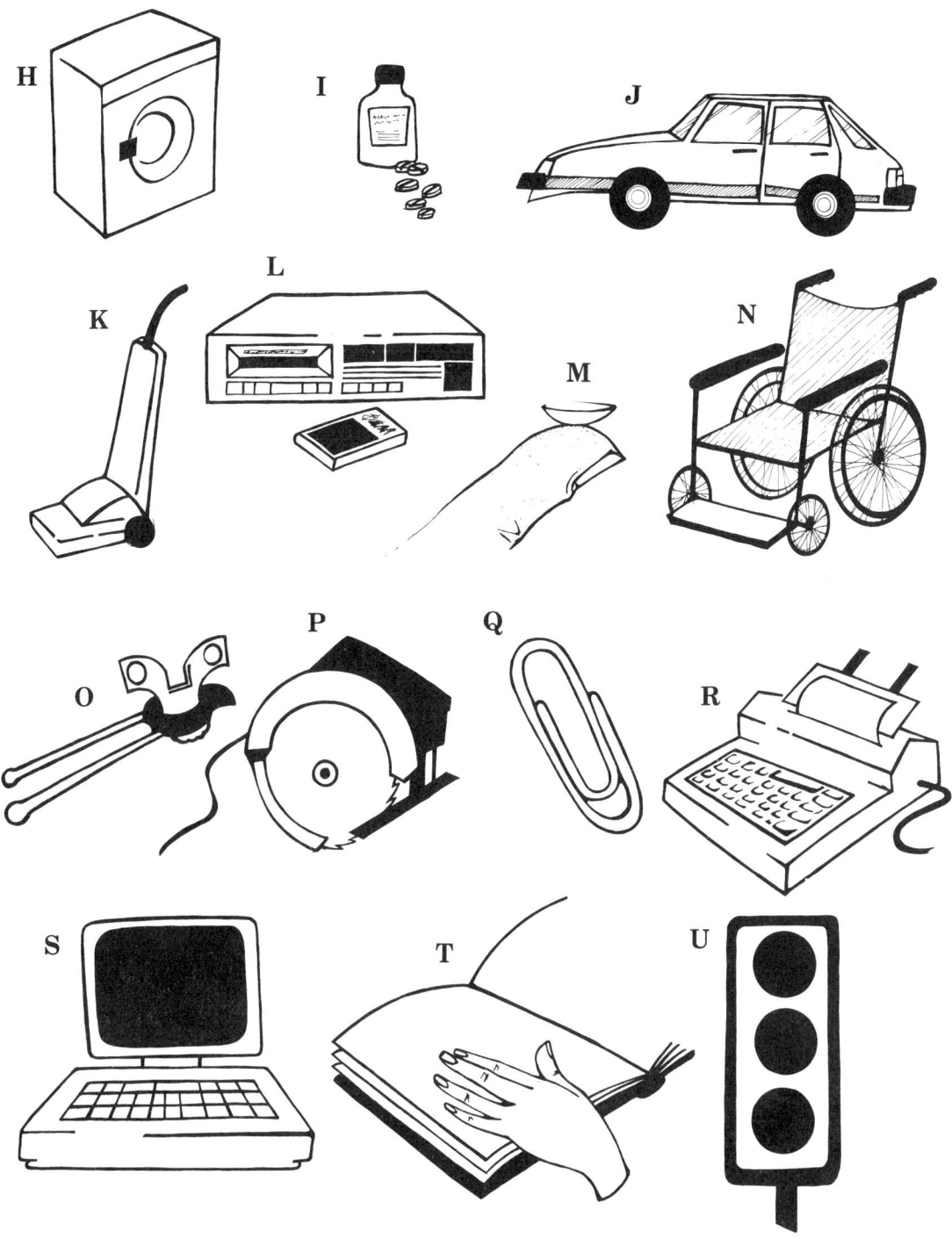

Weird Inventions

What to do
Match the inventions with their description.

1. This invention helps you with the decorating. It hangs the paper; then it brushes it into place.
2. This invention helps you to clean your tongue. It has a handle and a loop with bristles.
3. This invention helps you to get around in the snow.
4. This invention prevents ears sticking out.
5. This invention stops your clothes from getting dirty when you are cycling.
6. This invention stops an ill child from getting sticky medicine on the bed clothes.
7. This invention stops a pet making a mess on the carpet.
8. This invention helps you find out if you have bad breath.
9. This invention stops a man's moustache getting dirty when he is drinking.

What to do next
Look at this picture of an invention.
What do you think it is for?
How does it work?

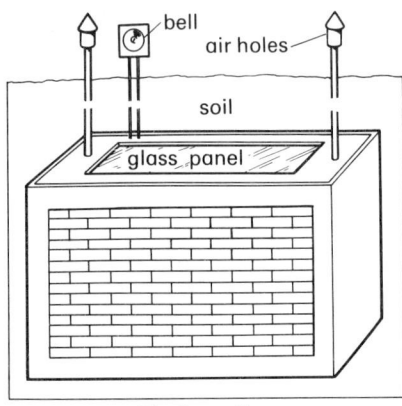

The invention

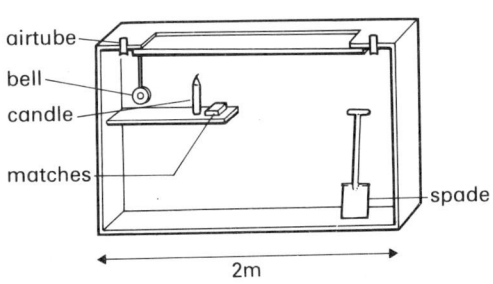

Diagram to show inside the invention

Inventions

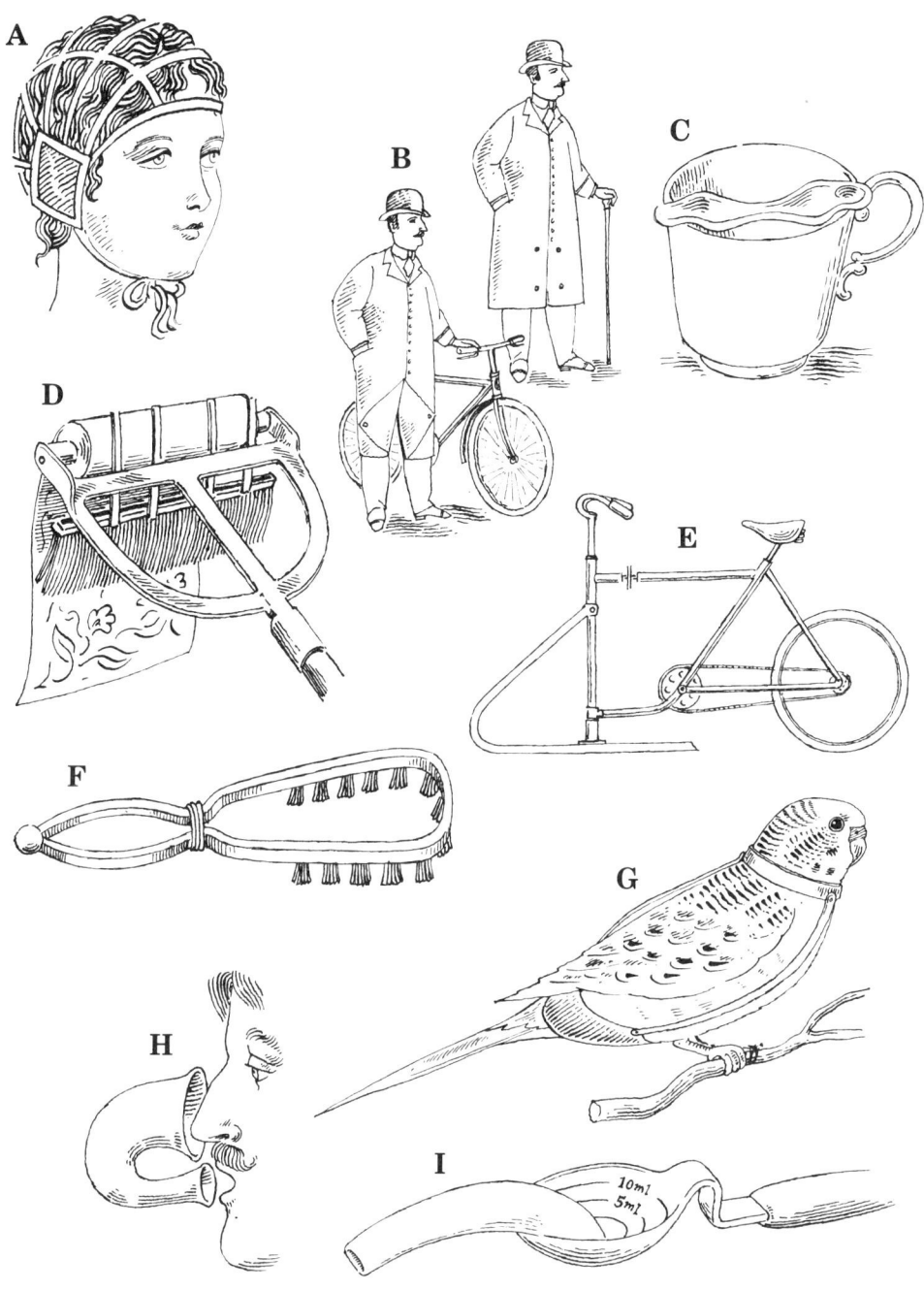

Inventions

From the Car to Nuclear Weapons

What to do

Read the sentences.
Copy and complete
the time line.

In 1897 the Kellog brothers made the first cornflakes. That was ten years after Daimler made the first car.

The motorcar was invented six years before the motorcycle.

The zip fastener was invented two years after the motorcycle.

The first domestic fridge was made two years after Birdseye thought of frozen foods, in 1920.

The first atom bomb was dropped in 1945. It was dropped forty two years after the Wright brothers flew the first 'plane.

Nylon was invented ten years after penicillin.

The first electric vacuum cleaner was made five years after the first 'plane was flown and two years after instant coffee was invented.

What to do next

Answer these questions.
Give reasons.

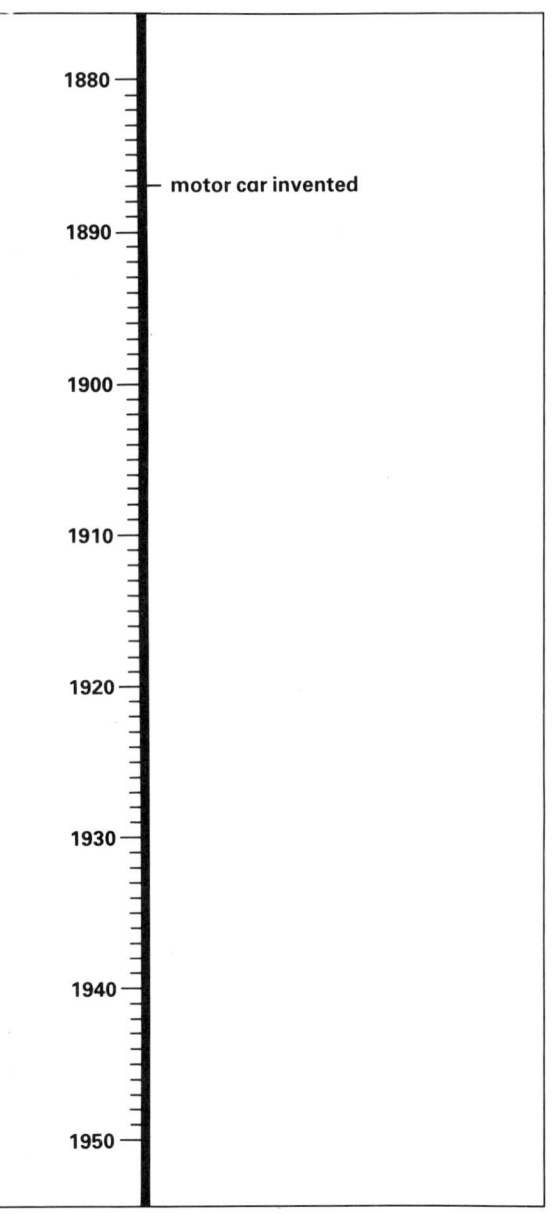

1 Which invention in the time line do you think is most useful?
2 Which invention do you think has killed most people?
3 Which invention do you think the world would be better without?
4 Which invention has brought the most changes in people's lives?

Classifying Inventions

> **What to do**
> Copy the table and put a tick where you think it fits best.

	Inventions	Used by you	Gives pleasure	Useful at home	Saves work	Saves lives	Can kill
1	Electric power						
2	Clock						
3	Vacuum cleaner						
4	Camera						
5	Paper						
6	Cats' eyes						
7	Cigarettes						
8	Gun powder						
9	Cinema						
10	Aeroplane						
11	Stereo record player						
12	Bicycle						
13	Motorcar						
14	Fingerprinting						
15	Wheel						

Inventions

— Important Inventions and Discoveries —

What to do
Match the ifs with the consequences.
Each **if** will have more than one **consequence**. You might need to use the consequences many times.

Ifs

A   If the wheel had not been invented . . .
B   If electricity had not been discovered . . .
C   If writing had not been invented . . .
D   If the motorcar had not been invented . . .
E   If the microchip had not been invented . .
F   If fire had not been discovered . . .

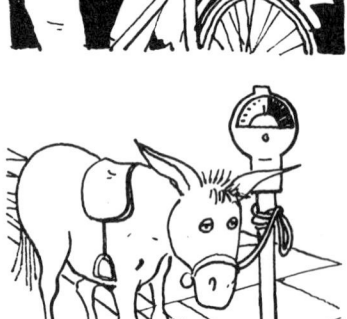

Consequences

1   people would have to eat raw food.
2   there would be no motorcycles.
3   people would wear warmer clothes.
4   there would be no postmen.
5   watches would be different.
6   there would be no computers.
7   there would be no central heating.
8   fewer people would go on holiday.
9   schools would be different.
10 there would be no street lights.
11 people would go to bed earlier.
12 there would be no iron.
13 there would be no books.
14 people would have to walk more.

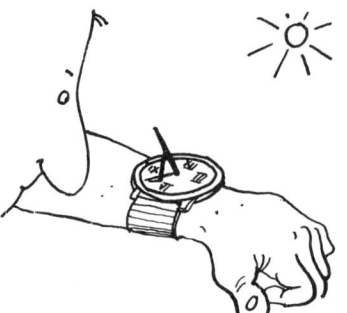

What to do next
1   Which of these inventions do you think has made the most difference to people?
2   What other important inventions can you think of? Give reasons for your choices.

Inventions

Computers

1. Computers and robots will put hundreds of people out of work.
2. Computers are great for kids to play games on.
3. Computers save time in offices and factories. They will give everyone more free time.
4. Computers will let the police know about everyone in the country. Soon there will be no privacy.
5. Computers can help the police catch criminals.
6. Computers are very useful in schools. They help pupils to learn.
7. My grandad got a gas bill for £2056,456.96. They said it was a computer error.
8. Soon there will be nobody working in banks. There will just be cash dispensers and computers.
9. Computers can help people who can't speak to communicate.

What to do

Copy the table and fill it in to classify the opinions.
Then write a paragraph to say what you think of computers.

	Good things about computers	Bad things about computers
1		
2		
3		
4		
5		
6		
7		
8		
9		

Mill Street

What to do
Are these sentences true, false or is there not enough evidence?

1. The chip shop is open every day.
2. The fishmonger is delivering fresh fish to the shop.
3. There are twenty-five houses in Mill Street.
4. The houses in Mill Street have garages.
5. Mill Street is a busy main road.
6. Mill Street is a one way street.
7. All the houses in Mill Street are in good repair.
8. A lot of old people live in Mill Street.
9. The woman on the corner is blind.
10. Nobody lives at number 20 Mill Street.
11. There is a newsagent's next door to the chip shop.
12. All the houses in Mill Street were built in 1980.

What to do next
Say how Mill Street is different from your own street.

Eric Collins

Everyone in Mill Street knew Eric Collins and everyone liked him. He had been born at number 22 and lived there all his life. It had been his mother's house. She was killed in an air raid in 1941. Eric was her only child. So the house came to him.

Eric never knew his father. Mr Collins was a regular soldier. He was killed in France in 1916, when Eric was only one year old.

Eric was always cheerful, always smiling and always busy. He got up at six o'clock every morning, summer and winter. He ate the same breakfast every day – porridge and a boiled egg. At about 7.30 he walked down to the corner shop for his paper. Everyone else in the street had their paper delivered, but not Eric! At about 8.30 Eric went for a walk along the canal tow path. He never walked far, but he never missed his morning walk – hail, rain or snow.

Eric had never had much education. He left school when he was twelve and got a job driving a pony and cart for the local baker. He delivered bread and cakes all over the town.

Eric's hobby was reading. He read about anything and everything. Because Eric was such a mine of information, everyone in Mill Street came to him with their problems.

"Eric, I've got bats in my attic. How can I get rid of them?"
"Eric, what's the best cure for hiccups?"
"Eric, how do you get beer stains out of a carpet?"
"Eric, can you help me fix a dripping tap?"

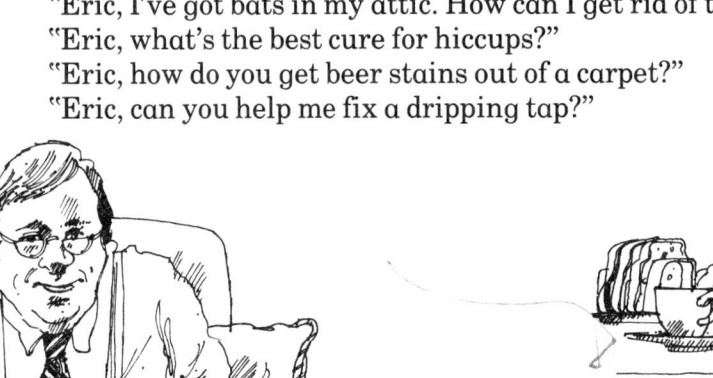

Whatever the problem, Eric always had an answer. He was always ready to help. The door of number 22 Mill Street was always open and the kettle always on the boil.

What to do
Are these sentences true, false or is there not enough evidence?

1. Eric was a very popular man.
2. Eric's mother was killed by a bomb that fell on 22 Mill Street.
3. Eric had two brothers who were both in the army.
4. Eric was 26 years old when his mother was killed.
5. Eric was in France during the Second World War.
6. Eric always went for his newspaper before breakfast.
7. After breakfast Eric went for a short walk by the canal.
8. Eric left school when he was twelve because he hated it.
9. Eric lives near the local library.
10. Eric always tries to help anyone who comes to him with a problem.

What to do next
Make a list of all the things that you think made Eric Collins a rather unusual person.

Mill Street

Eric gets a Shock

One day Eric opened the local paper and saw this article:

DRIVERS DEMAND LORRY LOCK-UP

Local lorry drivers want the Council to build an over-night lock up. They want to use a large bit of waste land by the canal at the end of Mill Street.

At present there is no safe place for drivers to park their trucks over night. Many drivers leave them on Canal Street. This upsets the local people.

A local driver, Jack Seddon, said today, "The land at the bottom of Mill Street is just what we need. It's near the industrial estate and only two miles from the motorway."

Mr Seddon wants the lorry park to have alarms, a night watchman, flood-lights and guard dogs.

"Local drivers are sick of vandals and thieves getting at their trucks," said Mr Seddon.

The leader of the Council, Jim Foster, said today, "We like the plan and we're looking into it."

Eric was very upset when he read the article. If the lorry park was built, dozens of heavy trucks would have to pass up and down Mill Street.

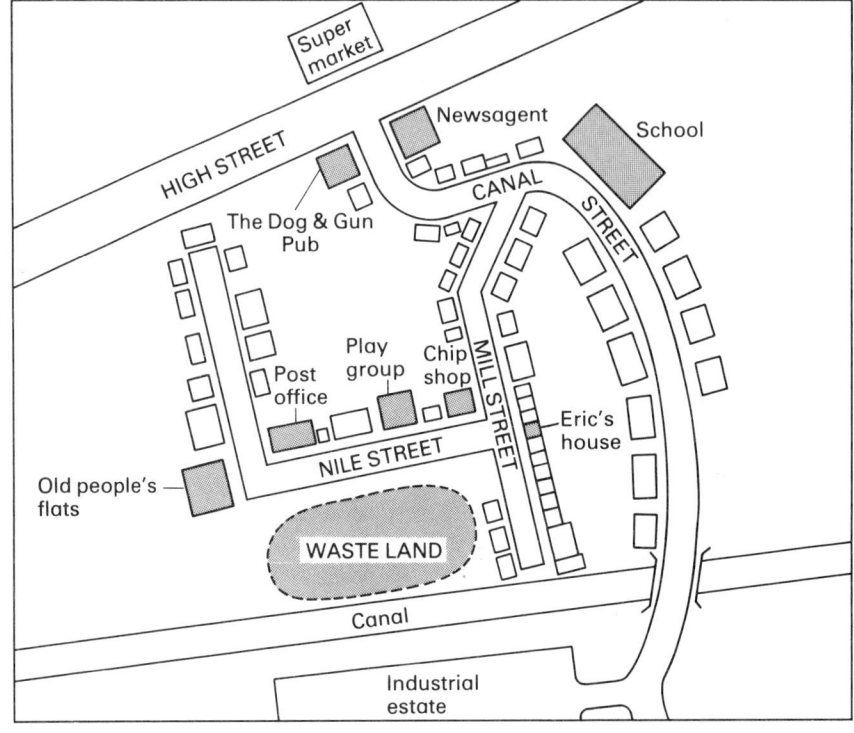

What to do

Some people want the lorry park. Some don't.
They all have different reasons.
Copy the tables and fill in the gaps.
The **map** will help you.

	People who want the lorry park	Reason
1		They want a safe place to leave their lorries.
2	The people who live in Canal St.	
3		The drivers would call in for drinks and snacks.

	People who do not want the lorry park	Reason
1	Eric and the other people in Mill St.	
2		The park would be very close to their flats.
3	The people who run Nile St. play-group.	

What to do next

When Eric read the article he decided to write a letter to the local paper, protesting about the lorry park plan.
Write Eric's letter.
It should include these words:

noise	danger	health	safety
fumes	children	old people	damage
road	houses	protest	action

Mill Street

The Protest Meeting

When the people in Mill Street heard about the plan for the lorry park they were very angry. Eric Collins organised a protest meeting at the Dog and Gun pub. They were worried that the plan for the lorry park would go ahead.

Here are some of the things that were said at that meeting.

20

Mill Street

 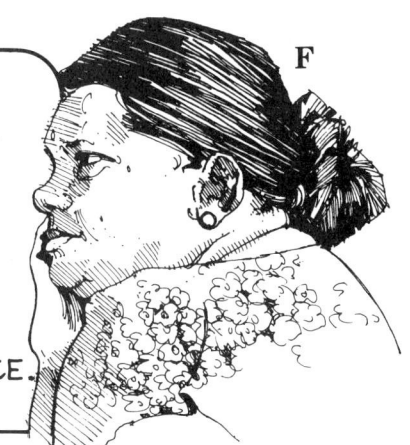

What to do

Copy the table and fill it in.

Protest	Lawful?	Unlawful?	Dangerous?
Person A			
Person B			
Person C			
Person D			
Person E			
Person F			

What to do next

Answer these questions.
1 Which of the six actions above do you think would be the most effective? Why?
2 If you had been at the protest meeting what action would you have suggested?

Mill Street

The Traffic Jam

> **What to do**
> Find the missing words. The picture will help you.

A few days after the ___1___ at the Dog and Gun, the people of Mill Street took action. At 9 o'clock on Monday morning they all met on the corner by the ___2___. Eric Collins had an idea. Everyone stood round and he told them his plan. There was a ___3___ crossing next to the pub. Eric said they should block the crossing and hold up the traffic on ___4___ Street. Everyone agreed. They formed a long crocodile and walked backwards and forwards over the ___5___.

Canal Street was a ___6___ road. It was used by all the ___7___ that went to the industrial estate. Soon there was a huge traffic jam at the ___8___ of High Street and Canal Street. Trucks got stuck on the main road and blocked the traffic.

One of the truck ___9___ shouted, "Get out of my way." Eric Collins said, "If there is somebody on the ___10___ you have to stop. That's the law!" The driver got very angry, but he knew Eric was ___11___. He had to give way to pedestrians.

So the people of Mill Street kept on walking backwards and forwards, backwards and forwards over the crossing. By ten minutes past nine the traffic was jammed solid. It could not move in or out of ___12___ Street. It could not move up or down ___13___ Street. At a quarter past nine the ___14___ arrived. A few minutes later ___15___ from the local radio and newspaper were on the scene.

> **What to do next**
> Describe what you think happened next.

Mill Street

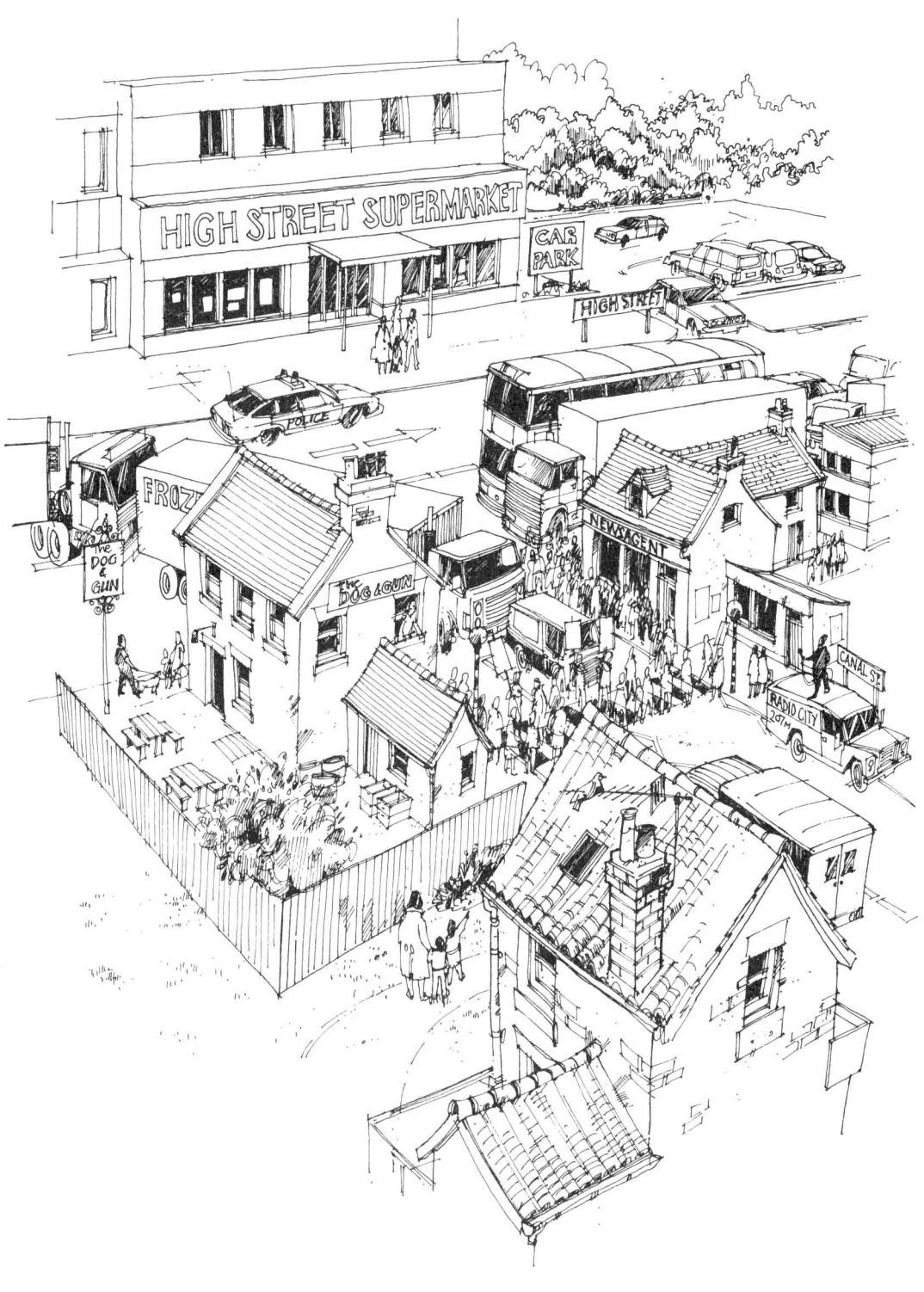

Mill Street

The Playground

After the protest the Council said they might not build a lorry park at Mill Street after all. Eric Collins had another meeting at the Dog and Gun. He said, "Why don't we build a playground on the wasteland by the canal?"

Everyone agreed this was a good idea. So Eric asked all the kids in the street for their ideas. This is what they said:

What to do

1 Make a list of all the things that the kids want in the playground.
2 Draw a plan of the kind of playground the Mill Street kids want. It should have a section for toddlers, a section for under 10s and a section for older kids. Label it clearly.

What to do next

Answer these questions.

1 Can you think of any other ways that the waste land could be used?
2 Do you think that the kids of Mill Street got their playground in the end? Give reasons.

GIANTS

Giants

Bird-eating Spider

The bird-eating spider from South America is the largest **known** spider in the world. The male has a leg span of 25 cm and can weigh over 50 g.

The bird-eating spider looks very fierce, but it is not dangerous to humans. Its venom (poison) is no more harmful than a bee's sting.

During the day it hides under rocks or in holes in trees. It hunts at night.

It does not spin a web like most other spiders. It jumps on its prey in a sudden, silent dash. It eats frogs, mice and small birds. It stabs its prey with its long fangs.

These fangs are hollow. The spider uses them to inject the venom into its prey. This venom turns the inside of the prey to a liquid. The spider then sucks the inside out of its victim – using its hollow fangs like a drinking straw. Female bird-eating spiders lay up to 1000 eggs, but usually only two or three eggs survive. These hatch in about 25 days, to grow into adult spiders that live about 15 years.

What to do

Are these sentences true, false or is there not enough evidence?
1. There are no spiders in the world bigger than bird-eating spiders.
2. The bird-eating spider's legs are 25 cm long.
3. These legs are covered with thick hairs.
4. A bird-eating spider can jump two metres into the air to catch its prey.
5. Bird-eating spiders sometimes eat frogs.
6. They trap small mammals and birds in their strong webs.
7. Bird-eating spiders are the most dangerous in the world.
8. Bird-eating spiders are very active during the day.
9. The female bird-eating spider lays thousands of eggs.
10. Some bird-eating spiders live for 18 years.

Giants

Robert Wadlow

Robert Wadlow was born on 22nd February 1918 in the USA. At birth he weighed 3.85 kg. He started to grow very quickly when he was two years old. By the time he was five he was already 163 cm tall.

When he was only nine years old he carried his father upstairs. His father was 182 cm tall and weighed 72 kg!

Robert was 210 cm tall when he was ten years old. By the time he was fourteen he weighed 137 kg and was 226 cm tall.

He wore size 37 shoes which were 47 cm long. His hands measured 32 cm from the wrist to the tip of his middle finger. His arm span was 288 cm.

When he died (aged only twenty-two) in 1940 Robert Wadlow was still growing. He was 272 cm tall and weighed 200 kg. He was buried in a coffin 328 cm long.

Was Robert the tallest person who ever lived? Nobody can be sure. The record books say he is **probably** the tallest person who has lived in modern times. Reliable records do not go back very far. There may have been other men or women taller than Robert Wadlow.

Giants

What to do

Copy the table and fill it in.

	Robert Wadlow	**Me**
Age	22 years	
Height		
Weight		
Shoe size		
Hand size		
Arm span		

What to do next

1. Make a scale drawing to show Robert Wadlow's height and your own. Use a scale of 1 cm to represent 10 cm.
2. You work as a reporter for a newspaper. You are sent to interview Robert Wadlow.
   What six questions do you ask him?
   Write them in your book.

Giants

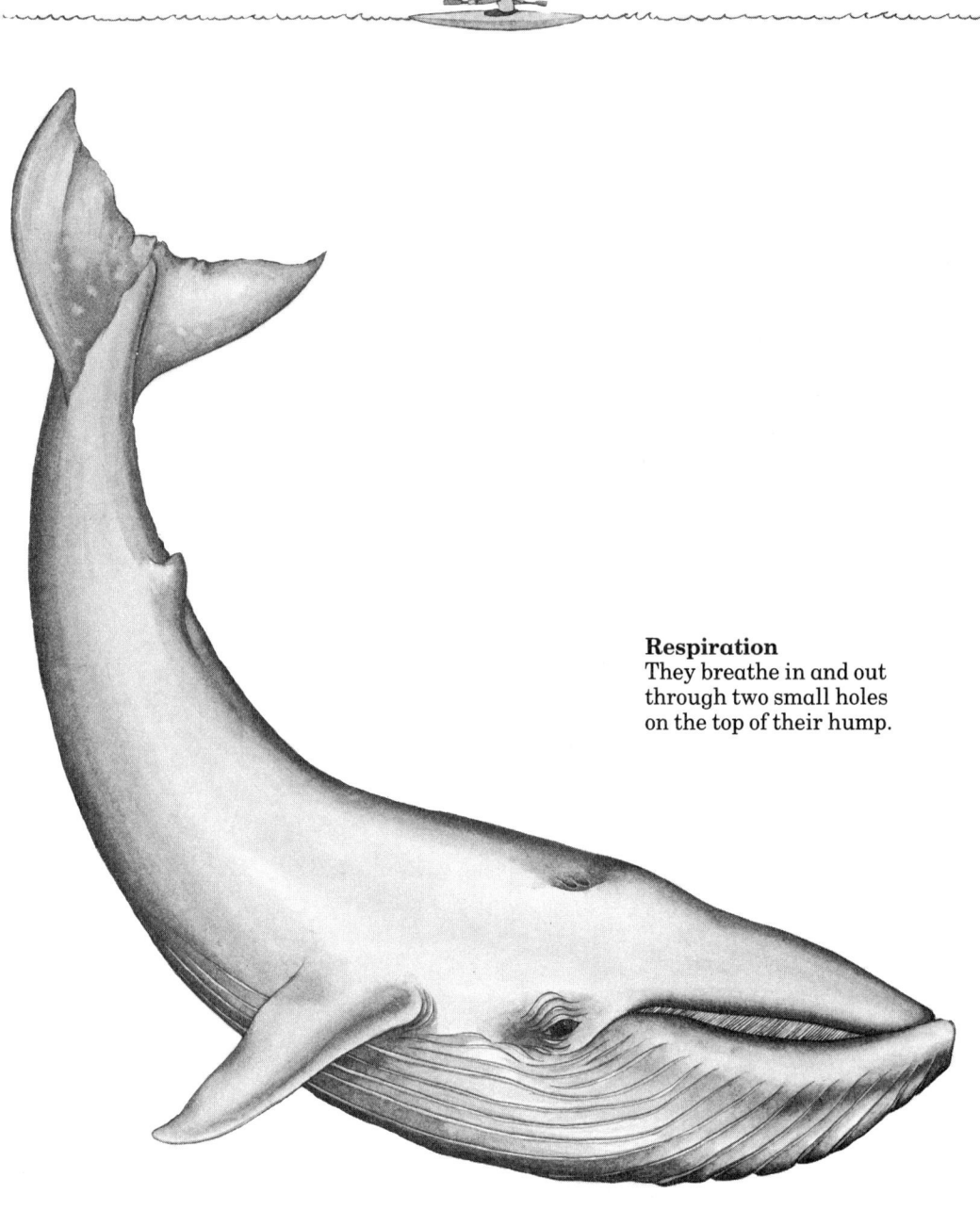

Respiration
They breathe in and out through two small holes on the top of their hump.

Giants

The Blue Whale

Blue Whales are the largest animals in the world. They are probably the largest creatures that have ever lived. They can grow up to 33 metres long and weigh 200 tonnes – that is as much as twenty fully-grown elephants or 2000 people.

Blue Whales look like fish but they are mammals. They are the only mammals that live their whole life in water. They have to surface for air. They breathe through two small blow holes (nostrils) on the top of their hump.

They have small ears, just behind the eyes. Their hearing is good but their eye sight and sense of smell are poor.

Blue Whales eat krill (a kind of shrimp). An average meal for an adult whale would be 2000 kg of krill. Blue Whales don't have teeth. They have a comb of bones (baleen) across their mouth. The whales suck in the krill like vacuum cleaners. Then they push the water out of their mouth and trap the krill behind the baleen comb.

Blue Whales rarely swim to British waters. The last Blue Whale was seen off Scotland in 1923. They live mostly in cold polar seas, but swim to warmer waters to breed. They do not have fur or hair like other mammals. Their bodies are covered by a thick layer of fat (blubber). This keeps them warm in the cold polar waters.

Blue Whales swim by moving their tails up and down. They can cruise on the surface at 20 km/h and will swim at 33 km/h if they are chased.

What to do

1. Draw the Blue Whale.
2. Label the drawing with information about the whale's vision, hearing, sense of smell, respiration, diet and locomotion.
3. Measure your classroom in metres.
4. Make a scale drawing to show the size of a Blue Whale compared to your classroom.

Giants

The Sears Tower

Sears Tower in Chicago USA is the world's tallest building. It is 110 storeys high and towers 443 metres over the city. It is the world's largest office block. It has space for 16,500 workers.

The Tower has its own restaurants, shops, pub, post office and bank. Two television stations and four radio stations transmit from the top of the Tower.

The Tower was opened in September 1973. It took 1600 workers four years to build. It has a steel frame weighing 76 thousand tonnes. This frame is covered in aluminium and tinted glass. This 'skin' has to stand up to rain, snow, hot sun and winds of over 160 km/h. Chicago is known as 'The Windy City'. In high winds the top of the Tower sways 25 cm!

The Tower uses as much water as one thousand average homes. It has 25 miles of plumbing, 1500 miles of electrical wires, and 145 thousand light fittings.

The building is 'barrier free'. This means it is easy for people in wheelchairs and other handicapped persons to visit the Tower. It has wide doors, ramps, special telephones and rest-rooms for the disabled.

A computer controls all the heating and lighting in the Tower. It also controls the fire alarms. There are smoke detectors everywhere in the Tower. If there is a fire, the computer will pump the smoke out of the building and switch on the water sprinklers in the ceiling.

What to do

Are these sentences probably true (PT), probably false (PF), definitely true (DT), definitely false (DF), or is there no evidence (NE)?

1. The Tower is the heaviest building in the world.
2. The Tower is owned by an American oil company.
3. The Tower is more than ten years old.
4. Most of the workers who built the Tower were women.
5. Most of the people who work in the Tower are women.
6. There are more than 16 thousand offices in the Tower.
7. The glass and aluminium 'skin' of the Tower helps to keep the building cool in summer.
8. The Tower uses one thousand gallons of water a day.
9. It is easy for a handicapped person to visit the Tower.
10. There could never be a serious fire in the Tower.

What to do next

It is the year 2086. You have just moved into a new flat. It is on the 1785th floor of a Super-city, a block of flats 2000 storeys tall.
1. Draw Super-city.
2. Describe what it would be like to live in a flat 4000 metres high.

The Hindenburg

The Hindenburg was the largest flying machine ever built. It was 245 metres long – as long as four Concordes standing nose to tail. Its volume (200 000 cubic metres) was greater than the volume of St. Paul's Cathedral.

It had four powerful engines and could travel at over 130 km/h. It had a range of over 5000 km. It could lift a load of 60 tonnes, including 75 passengers and about 50 crew.

There were 25 two-berth cabins for the passengers. There was a massive lounge, with a grand piano. There were kitchens, washrooms and showers. There was even a library. The promenade deck (used for sight-seeing) was 30 m long.

Travel on the Hindenburg was very smooth and quiet. The airship flew low and it was not unusual for passengers to hear the voices of people on the ground.

The Hindenburg was built in Germany. It made its first flight in 1936. It was used to carry passengers between Europe and America. In 1936 it made ten flights across the Atlantic. The journey took about 60 hours.

On 6th May 1937 the Hindenburg was coming in to land at Lakehurst, New Jersey. It was at the end of its long flight from Germany. It was thirteen hours late because of strong winds over the Atlantic.

The airship circled the mooring tower. The mooring team of two hundred men stood ready. The captain of the Hindenburg reversed the engines and the huge airship stopped. At 7.20 p.m. the steel mooring cables were lowered to the ground.

At that moment a shudder ran through the Hindenburg. Flames shot out of the tail of the airship. The tail section dropped and the nose rose 200 metres into the air. The stairways and walk-ways inside the airship acted like huge chimneys. Flames were sucked up into the nose of the airship. A great ball of flame shot from the Hindenburg's nose and the front section began to drop.

The mooring team fled in panic. The passenger cabins and crew's quarters were crushed under a mass of burning wreckage as the Hindenburg hit the ground. Sixty-two people survived the crash. One woman walked away from the twisted wreck without a scratch. A 14 year old crew-man jumped from the airship into a sea of flames and lived. Thirty-five people were killed.

Just four minutes after the fire started, the Hindenburg was a mass of twisted metal. Most experts think the fire was started by a gas leak and a spark caused by static electricity. (The Hindenburg was filled with hydrogen – a highly inflammable gas.) Some people said that it had been destroyed by a bomb.

At this time Germany was ruled by Adolf Hitler and the Nazi Party, who had many enemies. The Americans and the Germans investigated the crash. They both came to the same conclusion: the crash had been an accident. The cause of the disaster will never be known.

What to do
Copy the table and fill it in.

The Last Flight of the Hindenburg	
1 Date	
2 Starting point	
3 Destination	
4 Number of passengers + crew	
5 Weather conditions	
6 Time of crash	
7 Cause of crash	
8 Number of survivors	

What to do next
Imagine you were on the last flight of the Hindenburg. You were one of the lucky survivors. Describe your journey, the crash and your escape.
The table above will help you.
Illustrate your story with a diagram or drawing.

MOTORBIKE

36

Parts of a Motorbike

What to do

Match the parts of the bike below with the numbers on the drawing.

petrol tank
front suspension
front disc brake
engine
frame

rear disc brake
exhaust pipes
rear suspension
silencers

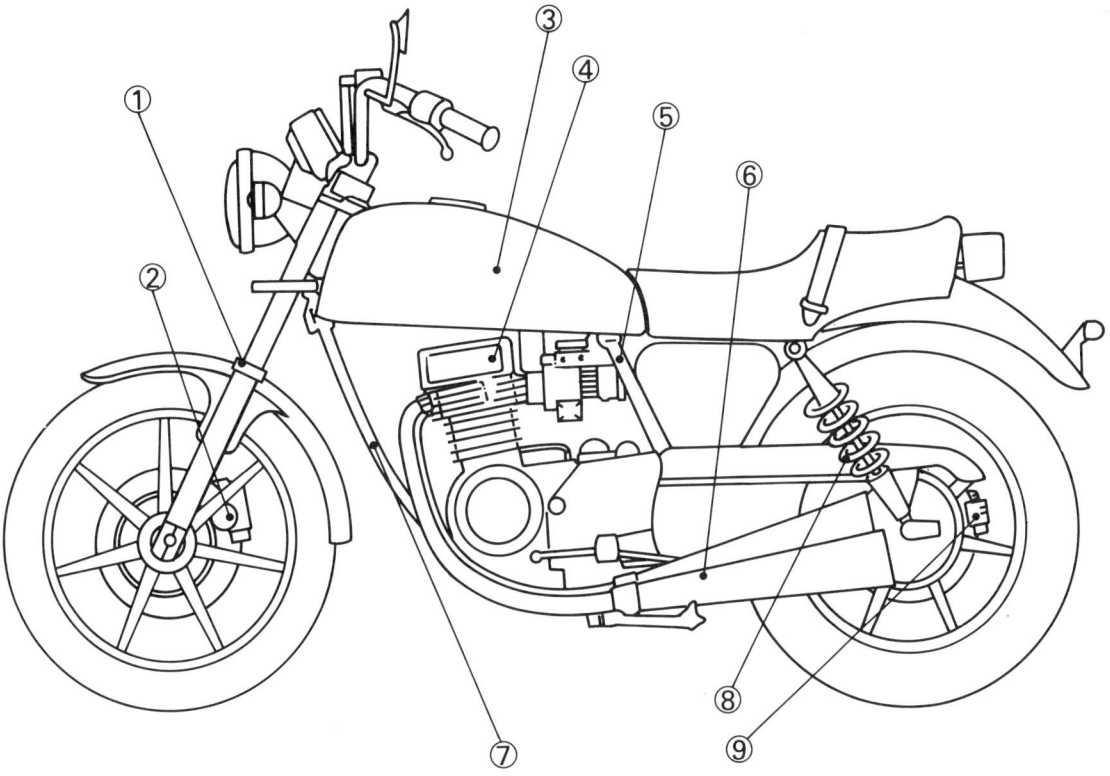

What to do next

Label any other parts of the motorbike you know.

Motorbikes Are Dangerous

> **What to do**
> Fill in the missing words.

Danger	How to try to avoid the danger
1 Motorbikes are unstable. When you are riding a bike it is easy to slip on oil or anything in the road.	Ride carefully and look out for ___1___ in the road. Never ride very ___2___ .
2 Motorbikes are small and difficult to see. Many ___3___ are caused when car drivers do not see a motorbike. This is particularly dangerous at ___4___ .	Always ride a motorbike with the ___5___ on even during the day.
3 A motorcyclist has no protection. A car driver is protected by seat belts and the car body. This is designed to protect the passengers. If you fall off a motorbike when you are going fast, your body bounces and bumps into anything in its way such as trees or parked cars. Your head may bang into something seven times or more. If you do not wear a crash helmet then you are very likely to get ___6___ damage if you crash.	Always wear a ___7___ to protect your head. Wear a good suit.
4 Riding a motorbike without ___8___ or a ___9___ can be dangerous. The wind pressing against your eyes can affect your eyesight. Stone chips can fly up from the road surface and can damage your eyes for ever.	___10___
5 Many motorcyclists are not very well trained. They can get on a motorbike and go on the road with no ___11___ .	___12___

38

Clothes

What to do
Read the passage about motorbike clothes and draw a labelled diagram to show what you think a motorbike rider should wear.

The most important bit of equipment for a rider is the helmet. This must be made to a British Standard. There are two types: full face or open face. A full face helmet gives better protection to the face in an accident but an open face one gives better vision. A rider needs either goggles or a visor. A visor gets scratched easily and will need replacing quite often.

A rider needs a suit. This ought to be waterproof for riding in the rain. There are two main types, nylon or waxed cotton. Some people think that an orange suit is a good idea because it is easy to see, but light suits get to look dirty very quickly. It might be better to get a darker suit and wear a reflective belt over it. The jacket should have a high collar and a belt to stop it flapping in the wind. It should have a waterproof flap over the zip. The trousers must not be tight on the knees or your knees will get cold. They must do up tightly over the boots.

It is a good idea to wear knee length boots. They can be made of plastic or leather. Warm gloves are very important. They must not be tight. The best are waterproof overmits with warm gloves or mittens underneath.

What to do next
Look at the picture of the motorcyclist. Write a list of the things you think are wrong with the clothes he is wearing.

The Argument

Keri Roberts wants a motorbike but her parents don't think she ought to get one. Keri and her mother are talking in the kitchen.

MRS ROBERTS: Are you going out tonight, Keri?
KERI: No, I'm going to stay in and watch TV.
MRS ROBERTS: What's up? It's ages since you went out.
KERI: Nothing, I'm saving up.
MRS ROBERTS: I hope you're not still thinking about getting a motorbike. You know what your dad thinks about that idea.
KERI: I'll be seventeen so he can't stop me. It's my money.
MRS ROBERTS: He's only trying to protect you. Why don't you save up for a car? They're much safer.

Mr Roberts comes in.

MR ROBERTS: What's all this about a motorbike? You know what I think. No daughter of mine is going to ride one and that's that.
KERI: Uncle Jack bought one for Kevin.
MR ROBERTS: He's a boy.
KERI: What difference does that make? He's a fool. He's always being stupid. He's a danger on the road but just because he's a boy that's OK.
MRS ROBERTS: You're right about Kevin. It's not because you are a girl. We just think that motorbikes are too dangerous. I wouldn't be able to sleep at night knowing you were riding around on a motorbike.
KERI: But Dad had one when he was young. He didn't have an accident.
MRS ROBERTS: Things were different then. There was less traffic.
MR ROBERTS: Anyway that's our last word. You're not getting a motorbike and that's that.
KERI: If I buy one with my own money you can't stop me.

What to do

Read the conversation and answer these questions.

1. Why isn't Keri going out?
2. Why doesn't Mrs Roberts want Keri to get a motorbike?
3. Why doesn't Mr Roberts want Keri to get a motorbike?
4. If Keri was a boy would Mr Roberts let her have a motorbike?
5. If Keri was a boy would Mrs Roberts let her have a motorbike?
6. Do you think Mr and Mrs Roberts should allow Keri to buy a motorbike? Why?
7. Do you think girls should ride motorbikes? Give reasons.
8. How could Mr Roberts stop Keri from getting a bike if she saved up enough money?

Motorbike

Please complete this form in **BLACK INK** and **BLOCK LETTERS**

About yourself

a. Surname **1**
   Christian or forenames **2**

Please tick box or state other title such as Dr. Rev.

b. Mr **3**   Mrs **4**   Miss **5**

Your full permanent address in Great Britain (see note on left)

c. Number and Road **6**
   District or Village **7**
   Post Town **8**
   Postcode (Your licence may be delayed if the postcode is not quoted) **9**

d. Please tick box   Male **10**   Female **11**

e. Please give your date of birth   Day / Month / Year **12**

f. Have you ever held a British licence (full or provisional)?   Answer **YES or NO**   **13**

Fees

Provisional licence
First provisional licence £10
Renewal of provisional licence issued before 1.10.82 £10
(Free for future renewals)

Full licence
First GB full licence £10

What licence do you want?

a. Please tick the type of licence you want (see note 'Types of Licence' on left, especially the one headed IMPORTANT under Provisional licence)

Provisional WITHOUT motorcycle entitlement **14**
Provisional WITH motorcycle entitlement **15**
Full **16**   Duplicate **17**   Exchange **18**

b. When do you want your new licence to begin?
A licence cannot be backdated.
You can apply during the 2 months before you want your licence to begin.

Day / Month / Year **19**

Your declaration

Warning: If you or anyone else knowingly gives false information to help you obtain this licence, you and they are liable to prosecution.

I apply for a driving licence

I enclose the fee of £ **20** (if applicable, see notes on the left)   Postal Order/Cheque no. _____

I declare that I have checked the details I have given and that to the best of my knowedge they are correct, and that I am entitled to the licence for which I am applying.

Your Signature _____ **21** _____   **Date** _____ **22** _____

42

Motorbike

The Letter

What to do

Keri's aunt in Australia sent her some money for her 17th birthday. This is the letter Keri wrote to thank her.
Use the information in the letter to fill in the licence form.
Write your answers like this:
Put a — if Keri would leave any box empty.

19, Longlands Drive,
NEWTON,
Lancashire.
NW5 6ZN

2nd September 1986

Dear Mary,

Thanks very much for the money. It will come in very useful. Has Mum told you I have been saving up to get a motorbike? Your money will go towards a decent suit so I won't freeze this winter. At first Mum and Dad didn't want me to get a motorbike. Mum thinks they are dangerous and Dad thought bikes are only for boys. I have persuaded Mum that I'll be careful and I think Dad has realised I'm serious. He is quite looking forward to me getting the motorbike. I think he is dying to have a go. I haven't decided quite what motorbike to get. I want the biggest one I can ride. I did think of getting a trials bike but they're no good for road riding and there is nowhere to go scrambling in Newton. I hope to have my new motorbike on the road by the beginning of next month.

I didn't plan to have a birthday party because I wanted the money instead. Yesterday Mum invited a few of my friends round as a surprise. We had jelly and ice-cream! It was the best birthday I've had since I was a kid.

Anyway thanks a lot for the money. I'll let you know all about my motorbike when I get it.

Love,

Keri

43

Motorbike

Choosing a Motorbike

What to do

Look at the pictures on page 36 and the specifications below. Read the passage "Motorbikes and the Law". Which motorbike do you think Keri should buy?

Motorbikes and the Law

1. Motorcyclists have to obey the same traffic laws as other road users. They must obey speed limits and other traffic signals.
2. Motorcyclists must wear an approved safety helmet on the road.
3. If a motorcycle rider is 16, he or she can only ride a bike of 50cc which cannot go faster than 30 mph.
4. When a motorcycle rider is 17 or over, he or she can ride a motorbike of 125cc.
5. When a motorcycle rider has passed two tests, he or she will be able to ride a bigger motorcycle.

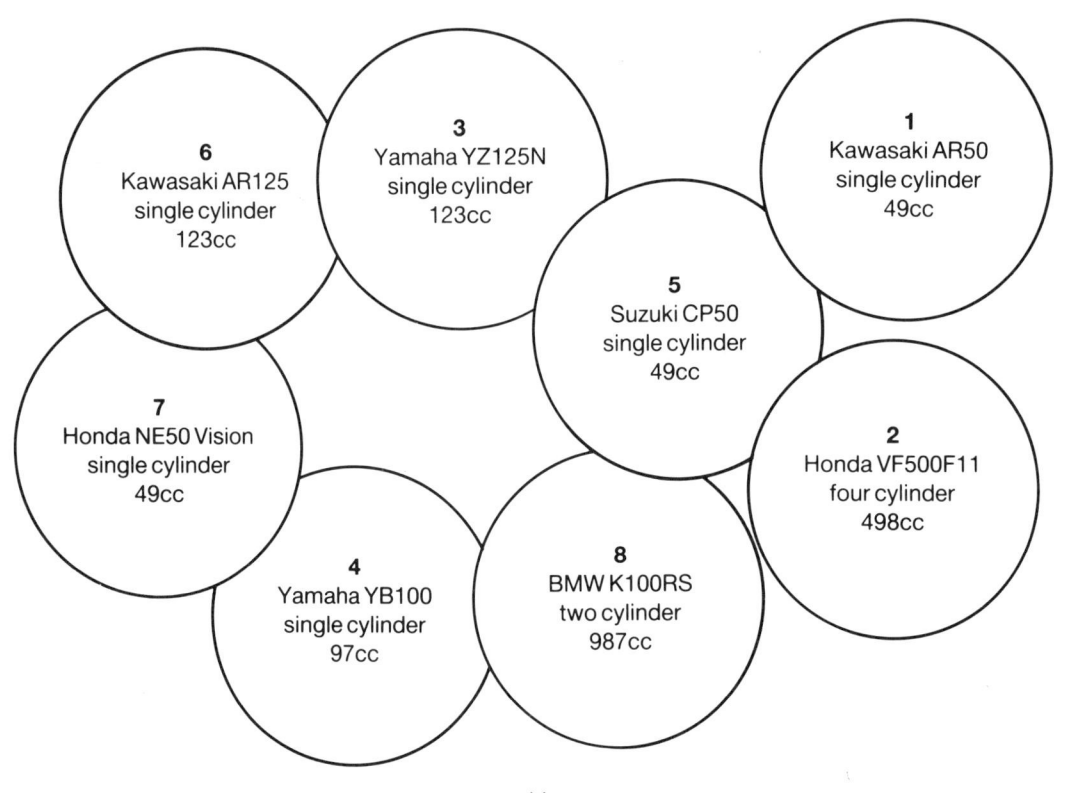

1 Kawasaki AR50 single cylinder 49cc

2 Honda VF500F11 four cylinder 498cc

3 Yamaha YZ125N single cylinder 123cc

4 Yamaha YB100 single cylinder 97cc

5 Suzuki CP50 single cylinder 49cc

6 Kawasaki AR125 single cylinder 123cc

7 Honda NE50 Vision single cylinder 49cc

8 BMW K100RS two cylinder 987cc

Motorbike

Kevin's Accident

What to do

The day after Keri got her bike her cousin, Kevin, had an accident. Read the description of Kevin's accident. Copy the plan and finish it to show how the accident happened.

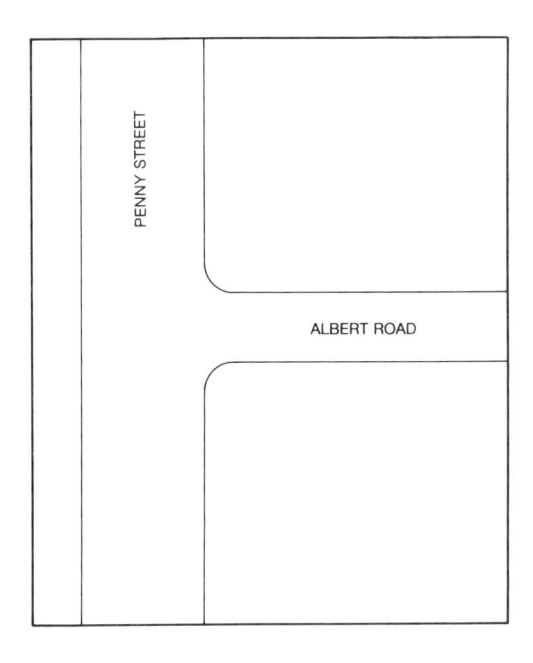

Kevin was riding along Penny Street. He wanted to turn right into Albert Street. He looked behind and saw a red van coming up slowly behind him. He indicated to turn right and moved into the middle of the road.

The driver of the red van saw what he was doing and moved to the left and started to pass Kevin on the inside.

Kevin did not know there was a green car behind the van. The driver of the car could not see Kevin and started to overtake the van.

The green car ran straight into Kevin who was in the middle of the road about to turn right.

What to do next

Write the conversation between Keri and her mum and dad when they heard about the accident. Set it out like the conversation on page 40.

LEISURE

The Leisure Crossword

> **What to do**
> This unit is all about what people do when they are not working. Some people spend their spare time doing crosswords. Here is a crossword all about things people do in their spare time.
> **Copy** and complete it.

ACROSS

1. What you call people who slide on ice.
3. If you are bored you might go to your friends for a _____ .
5. _____ spotters go to railway stations.
7. A coin collector wants coins in _____ condition.
10. Some people think this is cruel to fish.
11. You might get knocked out if you do this.
12. What you do to books.
16. The horse rider made a mistake at the water _____ .
17. You need muscles, wheels and a chain to do this.
18. Japanese self defence.

DOWN

1. Fish can always do this: people have to learn to do it.
2. This stops you getting wet when camping.
3. A racing driver needs a very fast _____ .
4. You might go to Wimbledon if you're good at this.
5. Most people watch this in the evening.
6. Where you find slot machines.
8. A bird spotter might watch this to see a bird come home.
9. "Eyes down" and you might win at _____ .
13. You'll find loud music and coloured lights at the _____ .
14. Something kicked in football and hit in hockey.
15. You can do this if you have a hang glider.
16. To run slowly.

Leisure

Fishing

Bream live in groups or shoals so if you find one you will probably find another. They are usually caught in still waters such as lakes or ponds. They are usually caught with a float and line.

Roach live in fast and slow flowing rivers as well as lakes and ponds. Most roach are caught with float and line.

Rudd look like a roach but they are more brightly coloured. They live in shoals in still water such as lakes or ponds. They are usually caught by float fishing.

Brown trout are game fish. They usually live in rivers. They should be caught by fly fishing. They are the only trout native to Great Britain.

Chub are large fish. They live in both fast and slow flowing rivers. Chub will eat almost anything. They are usually caught by float fishing.

Barbel are very strong fish that live in clean fast flowing rivers. They like rivers with a fine gravel or sandy bottom. Most barbel are caught by ledgering.

Dace are silvery little fish. They like fast flowing rivers. Dace are usually caught by float fishing.

Pike are the largest predators in Britain. They live in rivers and lakes. They grow largest in lakes. Pike are best caught with a spinner.

Carp live in still waters such as lakes or ponds. They can grow very big in the right conditions. There are three types of carp: the leather carp, the common carp and the mirror carp. These are best caught with a float and line.

Leisure

Bait

Maggots These are good for catching most fish.

Casters These are maggots which have turned into chrysalises. They are good bait for chub, dace and roach.

Bread This can be used in three ways. Bread flake is the soft inside of a loaf. It is squeezed around the hook. It is good for catching chub and roach. The crust of the bread can be cut off. It is a good bait for chub and carp. Bread paste is made by mixing water with bread. It is moulded round the hook.

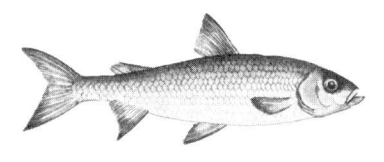

Cheese makes a good bait for barbel and roach.

Luncheon meat can be used as a bait. It will catch barbel, chub and carp.

Sprats and other small fish make useful bait for predators such as pike.

Spinners are used to catch the predators such as pike. They spin round to look like live fish.

Flies are used to catch game fish such as trout. They are made to look like real flies.

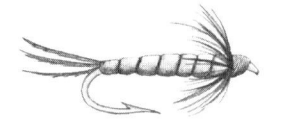

What to do

Copy the table and fill it in by reading the sections on fish and bait.

Fish	Where found	How caught	Bait used
Bream	still water, e.g. lakes and ponds.	float fishing	maggots

Leisure

Looking after a Pony

Feeding
1. A pony should be fed hay, greenstuff and concentrates.
2. If it is working hard, give it oats or nuts for energy. Don't give a young pony oats or it will become irritable.
3. Only feed it sugar or other titbits as a reward for good behaviour. Otherwise it might expect them and become bad tempered if you don't give it any.
4. A pony needs fresh water everyday.

Shelter
1. You can keep a pony in a field or a stable. If you keep a pony in a field it will need some shelter. A three sided shed is best.
2. If you keep a pony in a stable it must be at least 3 metres by 3 metres. The door should be about 1.5 metres wide. The door should be split in two so the top can be kept open for ventilation.
3. The stable must have straw bedding. The stable must be mucked out everyday. Dirty or damp straw must be replaced by clean, dry straw.

Grooming
1. A pony's hooves should be cleaned everyday with a hoof pick.
2. If a pony is kept indoors it needs to be groomed quite often. Brush it all over with a body brush. Brush the mane and tail. Sponge the eyes, nostrils and lips.
3. If a pony is kept in a field it should not be groomed. Just brush the mud from the coat and pick out the feet.
4. A pony will need new shoes about every six to eight weeks.

Exercise
If a pony is kept in a stable it must be exercised every day.

What to do

Read the rules about how to keep a pony.
Read the passages about how Ben, Samantha and Louise looked after their ponies. Make three lists to show what mistakes they made.

Leisure

Ben had a very young pony. He kept it in this field. Everyday he went to the field. He groomed the pony and picked out its feet. He fed it with oats and changed its water. He took it to the blacksmith for new shoes every year.

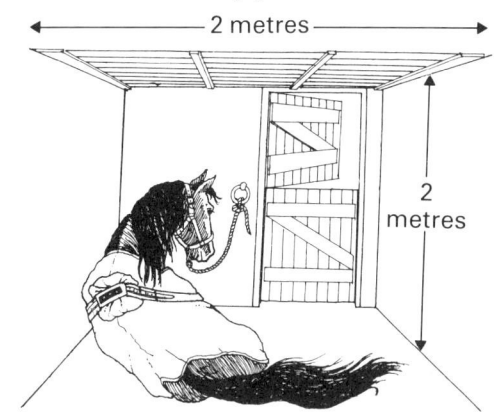

Samantha kept her pony in this stable. After while she got bored with looking after it. She only went to see it once a week. She got her brother to feed it every morning. She never groomed it.

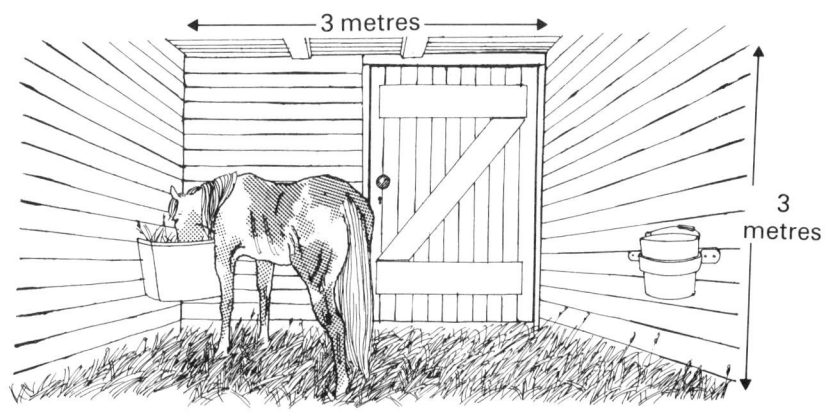

Louise kept her pony in this stable. She groomed it everyday and picked its feet. She gave it fresh water and mucked out its stable every week. She exercised it every day. She gave it sugar everyday when she went to the stable.

Leisure

Train Spotting

What to do
Are these sentences true, false or is there not enough evidence?

1. The 8.50 train from York to Manchester arrives at Leeds at 10.30.
2. It takes more than six hours to go from Newcastle to Birmingham by train.
3. The trains from Birmingham to York stop at Sheffield.
4. There is a buffet car on the 9.50 train from York to Manchester.
5. The train that arrives in Newcastle at 11.19 comes from Exeter.
6. The trains from York to Manchester go at 50 minutes past each hour.
7. There is a train from Sheffield to Exeter at 19.22.
8. If you travel from Manchester to York on the 12.48 train you could catch the 14.43 train to Exeter.

What to do next
Paula wants to go from **Newcastle** to **Bristol** via Birmingham. She wants to be in **Bristol** as early as possible. Copy the table and fill it in to show the times her trains arrive and leave.

	arrive	depart
NEWCASTLE	—	
BIRMINGHAM		
BRISTOL		—

Craig lives in Manchester. His hobby is train spotting. One Saturday he wanted to go to the Railway Museum in York. He also wanted to go train spotting in Birmingham. He had to be home by 8 o'clock. Draw a table and fill it in to show the times Craig would arrive and leave the station.

Manchester to York

Manchester	08.48	9.48	10.48	11.48	12.48	13.48	14.48	15.48	16.48	17.48
Leeds	09.53	10.53	11.53	12.53	13.53	14.53	15.53	16.53	17.53	18.53
York		10.25	11.25	12.25	13.25	14.25	15.25	16.25	17.25	18.25	19.25

York to Manchester

York	08.50	9.50	10.50	11.50	12.50	13.50	14.50	15.50	16.50
Leeds	09.20	10.20	11.20	13.20	14.20	15.20	16.20	17.20	18.20
Manchester	10.30	11.30	12.30	14.30	15.30	16.30	17.30	18.30	19.30

Newcastle to Exeter
via York and Birmingham

Newcastle	8.05	—	13.35	17.20
York	9.28	10.43	14.43	18.28
Sheffield	10.58	11.52	15.38	19.22
Birmingham	12.50	13.25	16.58	20.47
Bristol	—	15.00	18.29	22.20
Exeter	—	16.17	19.36	—

Exeter to Newcastle
via Birmingham and York

Exeter	—	08.06	9.31	—
Bristol	5.58	9.17	10.43	—
Birmingham	07.37	10.56	12.16	14.54
Sheffield	09.09	12.22	13.38	16.25
York	10.12	13.15	14.56	18.01
Newcastle	11.19	14.26	—	19.29

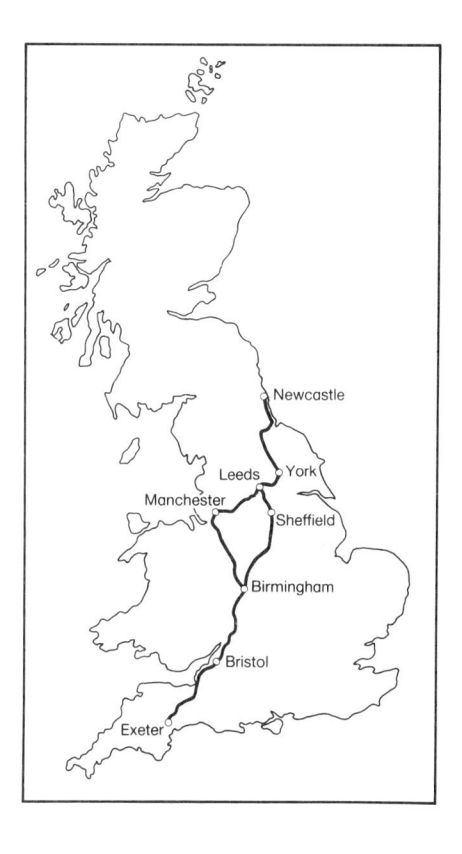

Leisure

What do you do in your spare time?

In 1948 thirty young people were asked this question: "What leisure activities do you do regularly?" The list below shows what they did.

Activity	Number
Cinema	24
Dancing	12
Youth Club	9
Church	8
Cycling	6
Watch football	4
Go to cafes/milk bars	4
Theatre	3
Speedway	3
Rambling/Hiking	2

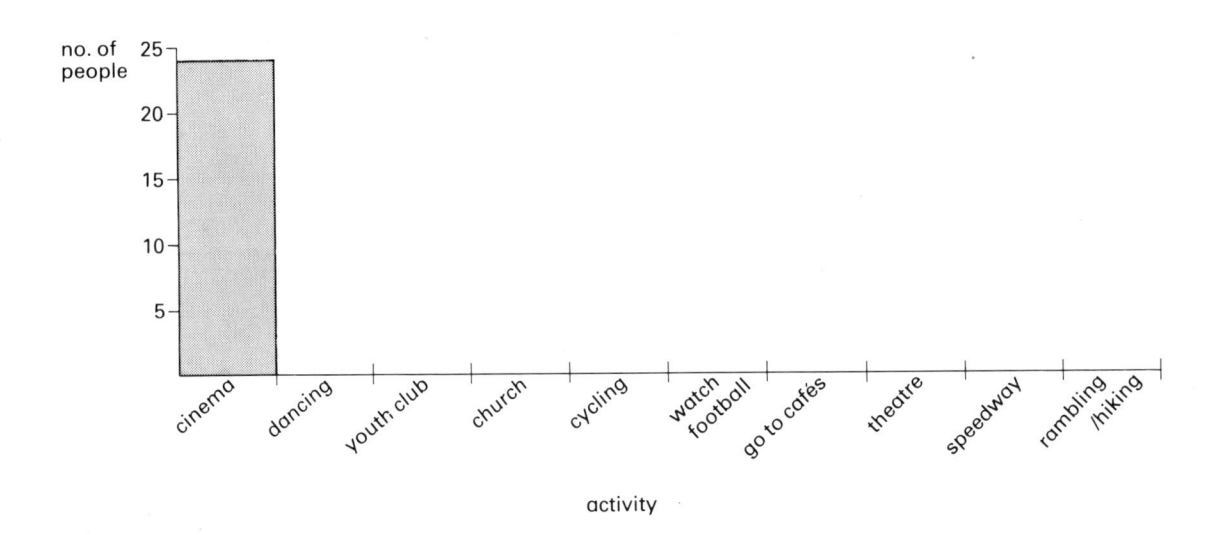

What to do

1. Copy the bar chart and fill it in to show the number of people who took part in each activity.
2. Which of these activities do you think more young people take part in today?
3. Which **other** activities do you think young people do today?
4. Do a survey in your class to find out what activities people do in their spare time.

Leisure

Cinema

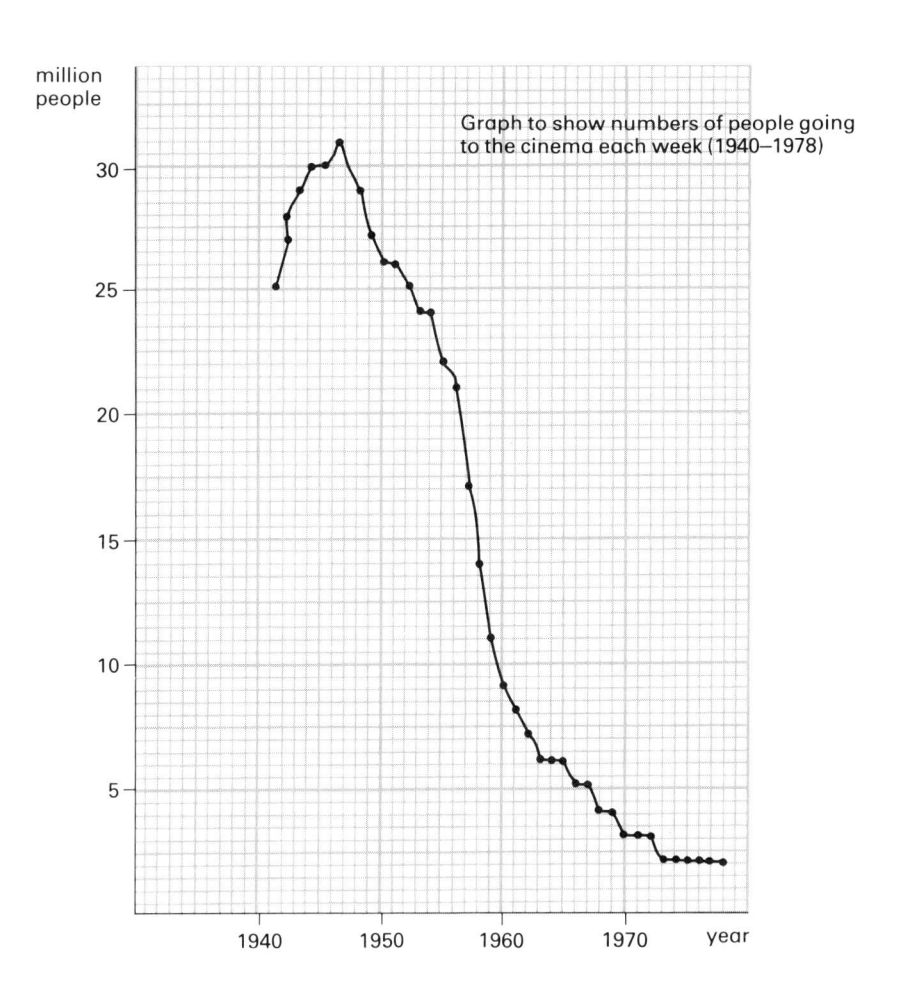

Graph to show numbers of people going to the cinema each week (1940–1978)

What to do

Answer these questions.

1. When did most people go to the cinema?
2. How many people went to the cinema in 1965?
3. When did fewest people go to the cinema?
4. In what year did 25 million people go to the cinema each week?
5. Why do you think fewer people went to the cinema in 1978 than in 1941?
6. Do you think fewer people go to the cinema now than in 1978? Give reasons.

Leisure

Classifying Hobbies

What to do
Read what these 15 year olds said about their hobbies.
Fill in the table.

My hobby is climbing. I first went with the school. Now I go most weekends in the summer. I usually go with friends to the Lake District where we camp. It's quite an expensive hobby to start with because you need all the right equipment.

I race pigeons in my spare time. I became interested when my uncle gave me my first pigeon. Now I have 10 birds. I keep them in the shed in our back yard. It takes quite a lot of time but it's not expensive.

I go to judo club twice a week. I'm an orange belt now. I started going two years ago with a friend. I just went along to see what it would be like. Before I started judo I was very shy. Now I feel much more confident.

I make models in my spare time. I started when I was about seven by building plastic models from kits. Now I build models from matchsticks. You can buy big bags of matchsticks from craft shops for next to nothing.

Leisure

> I spend quite a bit of my time dancing. I got interested when I was six. My mum sent me to classes with my sister. My sister hated it and gave up after a year. I'd like to go professional when I leave school. It will be difficult to make a living but I'm going to try.

> In my spare time I play in a band. I play the guitar and sing. My mum made me learn the guitar at school. At first I hated it. I had to practise every night. Now I realize it was worth it. We played at the Youth Club's Christmas party. Everyone said we were really good.

	Need to travel	A hobby you'd like to try	Can be done alone	Good for meeting people	Need to be fit and healthy	Needs expensive equipment	Easy to learn
1 Rock climbing							
2 Racing pigeons							
3 Matchstick models							
4 Judo							
5 Dancing							
6 Playing in a Band							

Leisure

A Sports Hall for Newton

Newton Council announced last week that they were going to build a new Leisure Centre. Councillor Houseman said last week,

"It's about time some money was spent on the youth of the town. Young people today have not enough to do. That is why they turn to vandalism and crime."

The Leisure Centre will have a swimming pool and sports hall for badminton, table-tennis and weight training.

At the moment the nearest swimming pool is in Olton, 2 miles away. Newton High School open their sports hall to the public but only during the evenings and at weekends.

Councillor Houseman said he would be interested to hear the views of any young people in the area.

This is what six young people from Newton said when they read the article.

I think the council should build a snooker hall. Snooker is very popular with young people.

I think there is too much money spent on sport. I hate sport. I think young people in Newton need somewhere to have a disco.

I think Newton needs a rollerskating rink.

I have got a motorbike. I think the money should be spent on a workshop so we can learn to mend our bikes.

Most of my friends spend their time playing in the arcades. What we need is somewhere else to go.

At the moment there is nothing for young people to do in Newton, so we wander around the shopping centre. I think we need somewhere to go where we can chat and have a coffee.

What to do

Write a letter to Councillor Houseman to tell him what you think of his plan. Use the ideas on this page and add any ideas of your own. You could use the survey you did on page 54 to give you some ideas.

Leisure

Some Magic to finish with

What to do
Read the magic tricks. Make a list of everything you will need to do each trick. Choose one trick. Practise it and then perform it to the class. You will need to think of some words to say as you do the trick.

The Safety Pin Trick

What the audience sees
The magician walks onto the stage and shows the audience two safety pins which are linked together. S/he shows the audience they are firmly joined together. S/he then pulls them apart leaving two closed safety pins. S/he then asks a member of the audience to come and check that there is nothing strange about the pins.

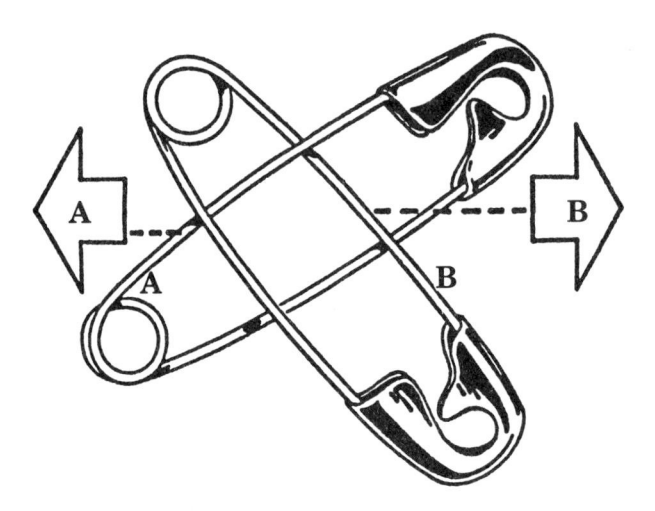

How the trick works
Join the pins in exactly the same way as shown in the picture. Hold pin B at the top and pin A at the bottom and pull. Pin A will open slightly and then close by itself. You will need to practise this at home until you can do it easily.

The Baffling Banana

What the audience sees

Ask for a volunteer from the audience. Give them a banana and ask them to check that it is a normal banana. Tell him or her to open the banana, over a plate. The banana will be already sliced.

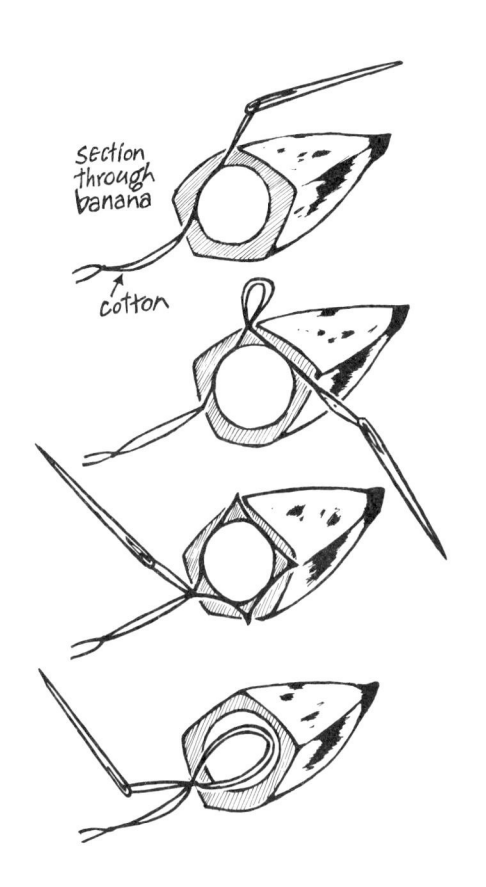

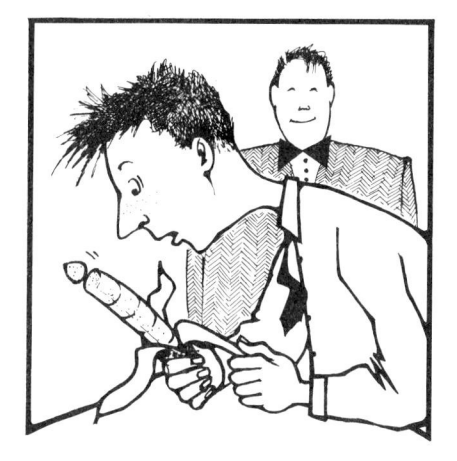

How the trick works

1. Get a fine needle and some thin cotton. Thread the needle. Tie a knot in the end of the cotton.
2. Pierce the skin of the banana with the needle and push it out of the peel a short way round.
3. Push the needle back into the same hole and push it out of the banana further round.
4. Repeat this four times until the needle comes out of the first hole.
5. Hold both ends of the cotton and pull. The banana will be cut but the peel will not be damaged.
6. Repeat from the beginning six times so the banana is cut into eight pieces.

Leisure

The Rabbit out of a Hat

What the audience sees

You come on to the stage with a hat and jacket on. You take off your hat and place it upside down on a table. You then take off your coat to show there is nothing hiding in there. You pick up your hat and turn it over. You pull a rabbit out of the hat.

How the trick works

Before you begin, put the rabbit in a special cloth bag which is hung at the back of the table by a large ring.

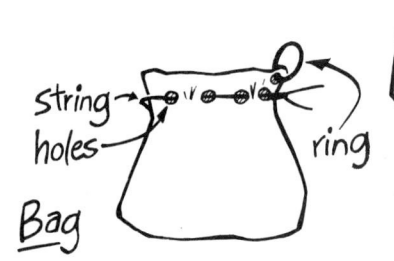

When you pick up your hat to turn it over, slip your thumb into the ring. Swing the bag into the hat when you turn it over.

Now you are ready to pull out the rabbit.
Use a **toy rabbit** or **soft toy** for this trick.

What to do next

Do you know any tricks? Write the instructions and draw some illustrations to show someone how to do your trick.

Talking Points

Inventions (page 4)
1. With a partner make a list of the inventions you have used today.
2. Give each invention on your list a score from 0–5 to show how useful you think it is.
3. If the inventions on your list had not been invented what could you have used instead.

Mill Street (page 14)
1. What do you like best about your street?
2. What don't you like about it?
3. Is it a safe place for young children?
4. Is it a good place for old people to live? Why?
5. How would you change it if you could?

Giants (page 24)
All the things in this unit can be found in the Guinness Book of Records.
1. If you could be a 'record breaker' what record would you like to break?
2. What is the most dangerous record you can think of?
3. What is the silliest record you can think of?
4. What group records could your class/set attempt to break?

Motorbike (page 36)
1. Would you like a motorbike or scooter?
2. Which of the motorbikes on page 36 would you choose? Why?
3. Why do some parents not want their sons or daughters to have motorbikes?
4. If your parents didn't want you to have a motorbike how would you try to persuade them to change their minds?

Leisure (page 46)
1. How do you spend your spare time in the holidays? In school time?
2. Would you like to do more? What would you like to do?
3. Either give a talk about how you spend your spare time: or give a talk about what you would like to do if you had the chance. Give reasons.

Note for Teachers

The **Headwork** series is based on the following assumptions:
> that we learn to read by reading;
> that reading is in essence a problem solving process;
> that different types of reading matter demand different strategies.

The books have been written to help pupils find a challenge in the necessary routine of practising basic reading skills and to help them understand that reading involves thinking. We have therefore tried to balance readability against 'thinkability' and posed demanding questions in an interesting but readable way.

English Headwork builds on the skills practised in **Headwork** Books 1–4 although the two series can be used independently. **English Headwork** presents a variety of tasks: cloze, matching, deduction, classification, drawing from text, centred on a range of topics. In this way the books attempt to bridge the gap between **Headwork** (a skill based series) and thematic based work in English classrooms. As with **Headwork**, the emphasis is still on developing reflective readers but **English Headwork** offers more opportunity for oral work and writing.

The writing tasks are all closely related to the unit texts and include: making lists/charts, writing cards/letters, presenting arguments for and against, as well as story writing.

Reading and writing skills are inextricably linked but we would argue that too much emphasis can be put on the latter. Genuine progress in writing comes only when pupils have achieved confidence and fluency in their reading. This is why **English Headwork** is primarily concerned to help pupils comprehend what they read.

Major skills emphasized	page number
Cloze	5, 22, 38, 42–43
Drawing from text	5, **10**, 24–25, 28–29, 30–31, 39, 45, **54**
Matching	6–7, ⑧–⑨, ⑫, 18–19, 37
Deduction	⑮, ⑯–⑰, ㊹, 27, 32–33, 34–35, 50–51, **52–53**
Classification	⑪, 13, 20–21, 28–29, 48–49, 56–57
Writing	⑤, 13, 18–19, ㉒, ㉘–㉙, ㉞–㉟, ㊺, ㊾
Oral	④, ⑭, ㉔, ㊱, ㊻, ㉠–㉢

Numbers in **bold** indicate tasks needing teacher explanation. Numbers circled indicate open ended tasks.